'A' IS FOR APPLE:

TEXTBOOK (VOLUME 2)

A
IS FOR APPLE
VOLUME 2

A primer by
WILLIAM D. WALTER

Wombley Press

© 2015 William D. Walter

Many of the images contained in this primer are in the public domain. All other material is original. No part of this book may be reproduced or used in any form or by any means without obtaining written permission from the publisher.

Volume 1: ISBN 978-1-943939-11-4
Volume 2: ISBN 978-1-943939-12-1
With answers: ISBN 978-1-943939-13-8

Contents

LESSONS

short 'a'   1
short 'e'   8
short 'i'   13
short 'o'   21
short 'u'   27
'ow' as in 'cow'   33
'y' (long 'i')   38
'ea' (long 'e')   43
'ou' as in 'mouse'   49
'th' as in 'bath'   54
two-letter words   62
'sh' as in 'shed'   67
'ch' as in 'chin'   73
'ew' (long 'u')   80
'oi' as in 'coin'   85
'ai' (long 'a')   90
'ee' (long 'e')   95
'r' blends   102
'ng' as in 'sing'   113
the suffix '-ing'   118

'ar' as in 'car'   124
'or' as in 'cord'   130
long 'a'   135
long 'o'   138
long 'i'   141
long 'u'   144
'aw' as in 'claw'   151
'ck'   160
'oa' (long 'o')   166
'igh' (long 'i')   171
'ir' as in 'bird'   179
ay (long 'a')   185
'oo' as in 'book'   194
'ow' (long 'o')   200
'al'   208
spelling rules for '-ing'   213
spelling rules for '-ed'   219
'er' as in 'butter'   229
'y' as in 'puppy'   235
'oy' as in 'boy'   247
'ind'   252
soft 'c'   261
'old'   270
'ea' (short 'e')   275
'ought' as in 'fought'   284
'oo' as in 'soon'   292
'le' as in 'kettle'   299
'mb' as in 'lamb'   304

'kn' 310
'wr' 315
'tion' 322
'wh' 327
'ies' 332
'ss' 337
final 'age' 342
'cious' 348
'tch' 354
'dge' 361
'or' as in 'motor' 367
'ph' 374
'qu' 380
silent 't' as in 'listen' 385
'eigh' as in 'neighbor' 392
'ture' 397
'ur' as in 'church' 404
soft 'g' 412
'oar' 417

POEMS TO MEMORIZE

A Chill · Christina Rossetti A-1
The Lord Will Provide · William Cowper A-2
A Morning Song · Isaac Watts A-4
The Seasons of the Year · Isaac Watts A-5
The Arrow and the Song · Longfellow A-6
There Is But One May in the Year · Rossetti A-7
Going Down Hill on a Bicycle · Beeching A-8

ing

taping   tapping
moping   mopping
hoping   hopping
liking   licking

Long or short?

1. stake ____

2. ruby ____

3. butter ____

4. baking ____

5. riding ____

6. supper ____

7. taping ____

8. cape ____

9. funny ____

10. super ____

Reading

Can I come shopping with you?
I was hoping to come.

Jess likes riding horses.
She is good at horse-riding.

Which do you like better,
biking or running? I like
running, but biking is
faster.

My brother likes baking cookies.
He likes making the batter,
shaping the cookies and
putting them in the oven.

What does it mean when
someone is fuming? "Fuming"
means "very angry." Someone
who is fuming is very angry.

Today we are raking leaves.
Raking leaves is something
we do every fall.

Exercises

1. Look at the piglet ____ its mother's milk!
   driving
   biking
   sucking

2. Don't look! No ____!
   peeking
   pecking
   picking

3. ____ at someone is rude.
   Sharing
   Staring
   Starting

4. Ned likes ____ on the trail.
   raking
   hiking
   wagging

5. They saw a poor man ____ for food.
   joking
   mixing
   begging

Stories

A Full Tub

My brother and I take a bath every day. Mother was still feeding our sister when we went upstairs to run the water in the tub. Mother then had us come downstairs to clean up the toys we were playing with before dinner. We forgot about the water running in the tub upstairs. We were downstairs a long time before thinking of the running water. We ran up the steps. When we got into the bathroom, the water was at the rim of the tub. It was about to spill, but we came just in time! I am glad we got there before it made the floor all wet.

We Can Help

Every day Mother cooks us meals. Every day she makes the beds, cleans our clothes and washes dishes. What can we do for our mother? We can do many things to help. All boys and girls can help their mother. Father helps our mother do these things, too.

Questions

1. How often do they take a bath?

    once a week

    three times a week

    every day

2. Why were they downstairs?

    to feed their sister

    to play games

    to clean up toys

3. Did the water in the tub spill?

    yes

    no

4. Did they get to the bathtub in time?

    yes

    no

5. Did the water make the floor wet?

    yes

    no

ed

plowed	waited
asked	needed
played	filled
rained	robbed
looked	stuffed
crowded	shouted

The farmers plowed the land.

Long or short?

1. cracked ____

2. lucky ____

3. gaped ____

4. trapped ____

5. runner ____

6. baby ____

7. tapping ____

8. rode ____

9. happy ____

10. stated ____

Reading

Will Mother bake a vanilla cake?
No, but Mother baked a chocolate
cake. Do you want to taste it?

Does Samuel cry when Mother
peeled the onions? Yesterday
my eyes filled with tears
when Mother peeled them.

Mom said, "This is beautiful!" Dad
said, "What is beautiful?" Mom said,
"This bouquet of roses is beautiful."

Leah raked the leaves. She rakes
them when the ground is dry.

Father told me to clean my desk.
I cleaned it this afternoon,
but my two-year-old sister
came in and messed it up.

Let me fill the tub with water.
When it's filled I want you
to take a hot bath.

Did Tom stop by? Yes,
he stopped by today.

Exercises

1. The bunny was ____ in the garden.

   hopping
   hoping
   topping

2. We saw a ____ at the zoo.

   tiger
   tigger
   bigger

3. The cat was ____ the milk.

   liking
   licking
   ticking

4. Bob has a ____ face.

   dale
   sale
   pale

5. The man walked with a ____.

   van
   cane
   can

6. Do you ____ to swim?
   lick
   like
   bike

7. Tom ran two ____ to his house.
   files
   mills
   miles

8. ____ up the pen on the floor.
   Sick
   Pike
   Pick

9. Who is that ____ at the door?
   raking
   taping
   tapping

10. The ship had a big ____.
    rudder
    putty
    ruder

Stories

The Rose

Elsa, a three-year-old girl, gave her mother a rose. "Where did you get this?" Mother asked, but Elsa ran away. Later we sat down to eat but Mommy got up and said, "I forgot to close the outside door!" Mommy went outside to get the mail.

Outside the door was a bunch of roses. A man had left the roses outside, but we had not heard the bell ring. A dozen red roses makes a beautiful bouquet. Who had sent it? Mommy read the note in the bouquet. It was Daddy who had sent the roses. Mommy counted the roses. One, two, three, four, five, six, seven, eight, nine, ten, eleven… There are always twelve roses in a dozen. What had happened to the twelfth rose? A dozen is twelve, not eleven! Did the man who made the bouquet make a mistake? Then Mommy had to smile. "Elsa, come here!" Mommy said. Elsa came and Mommy drew her into her arms and gave her a big hug and a kiss.

July and August

July and August are very hot months. We often go swimming, as it is too hot to do anything else. On the Fourth of July we like to see the fireworks. In August we rent a cabin in our state. By the end of August I want the fall to come. I'm glad when I feel the first fresh fall wind.

Questions

1. Who sent the roses?

   Daddy

   Elsa's brother

   Mommy

2. How many roses are there in a dozen?

   eight

   ten

   twelve

3. How many roses did Mommy count?

   nine

   ten

   eleven

4. Who was holding the last rose of the bouquet?

   Elsa

   Mommy

   Daddy

5. July and August are both ____.

   cold

   hot

   fresh

Syllables

1. plastic ____

2. till ____

3. running ____

4. play ____

5. pencil ____

6. drink ____

7. reader ____

8. pumpkin ____

9. oatmeal ____

10. sunrise ____

More syllables

1. ticking ____

2. pat ____

3. fill ____

4. printer ____

5. thinner ____

6. talked ____

7. cleaning ____

8. licking ____

9. packed ____

10. leak ____

er

flower	ladder	raker
tower	bigger	racer
copper	supper	paper
dinner	sticker	tiger
better	reader	Peter

What kind of flowers did you plant?

Reading

May I read that book
about flowers? I might like
to read it after dinner.

The box must be bigger
than that. If the box isn't
bigger, the stickers for Tom's
birthday won't fit.

Will we give Tom stickers
for his birthday? Why don't
we give him a better gift?

Tom's chocolate birthday cake
has three layers and has his
name written on it in big letters.

Must we give the cat more
to eat? I don't think so. The vet
said she's too fat and needs to
get thinner.

Mr. Litmer found the ladder he
was looking for. He lost it last
winter and didn't find it all year.

Exercises

1. The ____ will melt in the hot sun.
   better
   butter
   faster

2. We are late. We must run ____.
   fatter
   litter
   faster

3. Don't ____ the sleeping dog.
   cleaner
   bother
   teller

4. Although his older brother is a better runner, George is a better ____.
   swimmer
   runner
   hotter

5. Did you hear his ____ singing?
   thinner
   sister
   manner

Stories

Look at the Butterfly!

Edward and Tad see a butterfly. They try to run and get it, but it is faster then they think. They then get a net. Tad gets the net in hand and runs after it. His net swoops down, but it misses. Then Edward gets the net. He runs after it, and the net swoops down again. At first it seems as if he got it, but he didn't. The two stand back and look at the pretty thing fly around. It will never come to the boys. It is afraid of them.

Then the boys' sister comes out. She does not see the butterfly. And as she begins to speak to Tad and Edward, the butterfly lands on her arm.

A Car Stopped

A car stopped in front of our house. The car was stuffed with balloons. Mother looked at the man and wondered who the man might be, and why he had his car filled with balloons. The man took the balloons out of his car. He walked to our front door and slipped on the path. It had rained the day before and the rain froze in the night. The path was slippery. The man was not hurt, but "Pop! Pop! Pop!" went all the balloons. Our uncle had come to bring balloons to our house for my brother Micah's birthday, but now they were all popped!

Questions

1. Ted ran after the butterfly with a ____.

    stick
    book
    net

2. Did Edward get the butterfly?

    yes
    no

3. The butterfly landed on ____ arm.

    Tad's
    Edward's
    their sister's

4. Who was the man with the balloons?

    Micah's grandfather
    Micah's uncle
    Micah's brother

5. How many balloons popped?

    none of them
    two of them
    all of them

y

Billy	Bobby	oily
funny	belly	Becky
silly	soapy	chewy
puppy	baby	shady
Jenny	Kathy	softly
fluffy	Timmy	Andy
shaggy	bony	tiny

What was Billy rolling up by the shady tree?

Reading

It was a good summer, but too hot.
Although it was hot in September,
it will be brisk in October.

Becky took a trip to her
friend's house. Although Kathy
wasn't home, Becky spent time
with Kathy's mother.

Kathy's mother is a good cook.
Although she has many cook
books, she doesn't use them much.

Last November was Becky's
birthday. Kathy's mother took
the time to make Becky a cake.

Mr. Smith took a look at his son
Billy's foot. Billy's foot
was big and red. He slipped
and fell on the bank of the brook
by the house.

His son's foot got better
in a week. Although it was
a bit better in a week, he
did not play outside for
three weeks.

Sally said she will visit
Mrs. Wilson. Mrs. Wilson
has a fluffy bunny that
likes to be pet.

Tommy is happy to see
the new puppy. He and Benny
can play with the puppy.

It's such a foggy day
here in Pennsylvania!
It's so foggy, I can hardly
see the barn. Although it's
chilly, I have a warm coat.

My sister has a floppy doll
that she calls Anne.
I think it's an ugly doll,
but she loves Anne just the same.

The landscape of Pennsylvania
is very hilly. That's not so
in the Midwest, where my
friend Johnny lives. He says
it's very flat there. He says
we must come and visit
him to see his big farm.

Two ways to read 'y'

sky   foggy
daddy   jumpy
my   baggy
greasy   spy
cry   hilly
silly   try
easy   mommy
sticky   tricky
messy   fly
sloppy   sticky

Exercises

1. The meal was too ____.

   greasy
   silly
   happy

2. The candy made his hands ____.

   fancy
   sloppy
   sticky

3. The ____ began to wag its tail.

   sticky
   puppy
   silly

4. The joke was very ____.

   bunny
   silly
   candy

5. You need to fix your ____ hair.

   fancy
   hilly
   messy

Stories

It Is Easy to Clean

It is easy to clean. Many boys and girls think it is a hard job, but I think it is easy. When my room gets messy, I like to get it clean before I eat my breakfast, lunch or dinner.

Baby Jenny's Meal

My sister Jenny is a baby. She is not yet two years old. Last week, she had her first meal. Our mother made a mash of bananas and put it in a bowl. It was funny to see baby Jenny eat! She was very messy. She got food all over her mouth and cheeks. She had to have a bath in soapy water after the meal to get clean again.

I Peeked

I smelled something good! What was it? I went to the kitchen and peeked in. Mother had baked some brownies and put them on the kitchen counter to cool. They looked and smelled so good.

After the brownies cooled, Mother gave me one to eat. It was chewy and tasted very good. I like chewy brownies. Some boys and girls are picky about cookies or brownies, but I am not.

Questions

1. The boy or girl telling the story thinks it is ____ to clean your room.

   not good

   too hard

   easy

2. Baby Jenny is a ____ eater.

   clean

   messy

   chewy

3. It is ____ to watch Jenny eat.

   sad

   funny

   happy

4. The brownies were ____.

   oily

   soapy

   chewy

5. Is the story teller picky?

   yes

   no

Poetry

Swinging
By Lucy Clifford

Swing, swing, swing,
Through the drowsy afternoon;
Swing, swing, swing,
Up I go to meet the moon.
Swing, swing, swing,
I can see as I go high
Far along the **crimson** sky;
I can see as I come down
The tops of houses in the town;
High and low,
Fast and slow,
Swing, swing, swing.

Swing, swing, swing,
See! the sun is gone away;
Swing, swing, swing,
Gone to make a bright new day.
Swing, swing, swing.
I can see as up I go

The poplars waving to and fro,
I can see as I come down
The lights are twinkling in the town,
High and low,
Fast and slow,
Swing, swing, swing.

Questions

1. What does the "crimson" mean? (It is printed in bold in the reading.)

   red

   fast

   sad

2. A stanza is a part of a poem. Stanzas are printed with space in between them. There are two stanzas in this poem. The first stanza talks about swinging ____.

   in the daytime

   at night

   in the early morning

3. The second stanza talks about swinging in ____.

   in the daytime
   at night
   in the early morning

4. What is NOT talked about in the first stanza?

   swinging
   seeing tops of houses
   playing with friends

5. What is NOT talked about in the second stanza?

   going home
   trees
   lights in the town

oy

boy	soy	cloy
toy	coy	enjoy
Roy	joy	annoy

Roy gave the boy something to eat.

Reading

What did Tom give to the boys?
Was it their toy? No, I think it
was a new shoe.

Roy is a friend. He and I often
play with our toys in our yard.

What is a ploy? Kate and
Andy asked me what "ploy"
means. I will tell them.

A ploy is a plan.
What was the boy's ploy?
His ploy was to trick Jill.

Did Rebecca get a new toy? Yes,
she got a new toy. I saw the joy
on her face when she got the toy.

It was such a joy to see
the eagle fly into the sky.
Did you see it?

It was a great joy to see the
birds build their nests there.

Does what he says annoy you?
He does not annoy me.

Exercises

1. It is not good to ____ your brother or sister.
   soy
   boy
   annoy

2. ____ beans are eaten in China.
   Soy
   Coy
   Roy

3. Henry ____ playing chess.
   cloys
   ploys
   enjoys

4. What a ____ to see you again!
   joy
   coy
   toy

5. Please clean up your ____, Emily.
   joys
   toys
   soys

Stories

Did It Cloy?

Did you eat too much? When we eat too much of any one thing, it will cloy. If you eat great mounds of cream with anything, you will get sick. If you eat a pound of nuts, you will get sick, too. Too much cream or a lot of nuts will cloy.

Ships Ahoy!

"Ship ahoy! Ship ahoy!" Is that what the man says when he is at sea? "Ship ahoy"?

Toys

Toys are fun. It is good for a boy or girl to have toys. What toys do you like?

What I Plan

Sometimes I think I will build some great thing. This is a plan that I have. I will build some great thing that will help man.

Questions

1. If we eat too much cream, it will ____.
   be good
   cloy
   be a nut

2. If you eat a pound of cream, you will get ____.
   bad
   good
   sick

3. Men at sea say "____" if they see a ship.
   Look, a ship!
   It's a boy!
   Ship ahoy!

4. It is ____ for boys and girls to have toys.
   bad
   good
   sad

5. What is his plan?
   He has a plan to build some bad thing.
   He has a plan to get sick.
   He has a plan to help.

ind

find bind
mind kind
rind grind
wind blind
hind behind

Look at the hind
leap over the branch!

Reading

The kind man said, "Do you
mind if I sit here? I need
to wait for the bus to come."

We saw the blind woman
cross the street. She was
carrying a white cane.

Elias and Anna said that they
do not know what the word "hind"
means. Mr. Walter told them that
the word means a wild deer.

I saw a hind leap across this field.
It was a great joy to see.
Do you want to see it, too?

If you grind this grain, you will
have flour to bake some bread.
The flour will be fresh.

Is the child going to run
the race? Yes, The child will
run in the race today.

Did Ruth find her pen?
If she finds the pen, let me know.

Exercises

1. Sam, did you ____ your hat?

   find
   hind
   mind

2. Tom's father is a ____ man.

   kind
   blind
   grind

3. ____ up the top and then let it spin.

   Mind
   Wind
   Kind

4. We do things with our hands and think with our ____.

   rind
   bind
   mind

5. Can we eat the ____ of the orange?

   blind
   rind
   find

6. Did Kate help the ____ find her toy?

wild

grind

child

7. Has the dog hurt its ____ leg?

rind

hind

mind

8. Did you remember to ____ up the clock?

find

mind

wind

9. Jim did not eat the ____ of the orange.

bind

rind

grind

10. Let me take these papers and ____ them with a staple.

grind

bind

find

11. The tool will ____ the stone into powder.

    bind
    grind
    wind

12. In the woods there are many ____ beasts.

    wild
    rind
    grind

13. I did not ____ what I was looking for.

    wild
    find
    child

14. We think with our ____.

    rinds
    finds
    minds

15. He was an old man, but very ____.

    childlike
    grind
    wind

16. A lost hat

   find
   blind
   rind

17. Not using eyes

   rind
   wind
   blind

18. A sheaf of wheat

   bind
   rind
   mind

19. Thinking

   mind
   wind
   bind

20. Back legs

   hind
   rind
   mind

Stories

King Solomon

I like reading about Solomon. Solomon was a very wise king. Did you know that when God said to him, "Ask what I shall give thee"? Solomon asked for wisdom. Solomon did not ask for a long life. He did not ask to be rich. Yes, he said to God, "Give me a wise mind." Did God give him a wise mind? Yes, he did. But God gave him not just a wise mind, but also made him rich. Solomon became so wise and rich that the Queen of Sheba came to see. Did she see it? Yes, she did. She left, saying that Solomon was wiser and richer than she had heard.

Orange Rind

The skin of an orange is called a rind. Can we eat the rind of an orange? We can shred the rind and put it in pies or cakes. When you shred it, the tasty orange peel is called zest.

Questions

1. Solomon was ____.

    the Queen of Sheba
    not rich
    a wise king

2. What did Solomon ask God for?

    a wise mind
    riches
    a queen

3. Who came to see Solomon?

    a king
    a queen
    a bad man

4. Why did the Queen of Sheba go to see Solomon?

    She wanted to see if he was really wise and rich.
    She wanted to see if she liked his kingdom.
    She feared what he would do if she did not see him.

5. What do you do with orange rind?

    You eat it plain.
    You shred it and put it in pies or cakes.
    You cannot eat it, so you must throw it out.

Contractions

wouldn't	haven't
couldn't	shouldn't
shouldn't	wouldn't
haven't	couldn't
wouldn't	hasn't
hasn't	haven't
couldn't	shouldn't
shouldn't	haven't
hasn't	wouldn't
wouldn't	shouldn't
couldn't	haven't
shouldn't	couldn't
wouldn't	shouldn't

soft c

pace	face	trace
mice	lace	grace
rice	race	icing
lice	spice	racing
nice	space	tracing
ice	price	center

Did the people walk at a fast pace?

Reading

All our eyes were on Mommy's
fresh loaf. Could we have some
now? No, the loaf is too hot to slice.

Micah thinks we are having rice
and beans for dinner. Samuel
likes rice with a lot of spice.

Let's have a bike race!
I will race you to the end
of the dirt road! My brother
showed me how to ride a bike
eight weeks ago.

The barn has a lot of mice.
Did you see Emma's face
when I caught eight mice
from under the hay?

I need some more space
on the desk to write my letter.
I am writing a letter to Catherine.

Did you draw that lion, Jim,
or did you trace it?

Exercises

1. Emily, did you ____ the loaf?

    mice
    rice
    slice

2. Wash your ____!

    rice
    space
    face

3. The ____ makes the dress look pretty.

    lace
    rice
    nice

4. The people ate ____ and beans for dinner.

    rice
    mice
    pace

5. The girl with a broken leg wore a ____ to walk.

    nice
    brace
    pace

6. The rocket went into deep, black ____.

   lice
   face
   space

7. Did his sister Anna ____ that picture?

   trace
   pace
   grace

8. Jill will be running in the ____.

   race
   lice
   rice

9. God is good and full of ____.

   grace
   face
   space

10. Bobby, be ____ to your brother.

    race
    nice
    pace

11. A pest that likes to eat cheese
    mice
    rice
    slice

12. Stars in the sky
    rice
    space
    face

13. Food in Japan
    lace
    rice
    nice

14. Fancy gowns and dresses
    lace
    mice
    place

15. A broken leg
    nice
    brace
    pace

Stories

Smiling Eyes

I like to look at the face of people that I meet. Why? Because their eyes will tell me much about them. Sometimes they smile, and sometimes they don't. Sometimes when there is no smile on the mouth, there is one in the eyes!

The Girl's Dress

The girl's dress had lace. Hannah thinks that the white lace makes the blue dress look pretty. I think so, too. But Edward does not think so. Why doesn't he? He does not like lace or anything nice. Boys, he says, do not like those things. What do you think?

Elsa's Messy Face

I know what baby Elsa had for dinner. She had rice with some red sauce. She also had two chocolate chip cookies for dessert. I didn't see her eat dinner, but I know what she ate. How do I know? Her face tells all!

I Like to Trace

On Saturday I like to trace planes from a book. The book has nice big black and white drawings of eight new planes. The paper I use is very thin and makes it easy to trace. Bruce taught me how to trace last year.

Mice

Some people are scared of mice, but I'm not. Last week I saw eight mice come into the kitchen. My Aunt Grace, who was visiting us, started to scream. I closed my eyes and picked the mice up by their tails. Aunt Grace didn't stop screaming until I took them outside. Aunt Grace made me wash my hands for ten minutes, I think.

Questions

1. Sometimes our ____ can "smile."

   eyes

   hair

   hands

2. Hannah thinks that the lace on the blue dress looks ____.

   rich

   pretty

   bad

3. Elsa had ____ for dinner.

   beans

   ham

   rice

4. How did Elsa's face tell what she had eaten?

   She had sauce on her face.

   She was smiling.

   She looked sad.

5. Why did Aunt Grace scream?

   She was scared of mice.

   She was sad.

   She liked mice.

Poetry

Two Pigeons

I had two pigeons bright and gay,
They flew from me the other day.
What was the reason they did go?
I cannot tell, for I do not know.

Questions

1. A pigeon is a ____.

    cow
    bird
    plane

2. Does the speaker know why the pigeon went away?

    yes
    no

old

old
fold
mold
sold
cold
bold
told
hold
folder
holder
coldest
older

The old man leaned on his cane.

Reading

What month is the coldest
month where you live?
Is it January or February?

Is there a holiday in January?
Yes, there is. New Year's Day
is on the first day of January.

February is the shortest month.
In most years, February has 28
days, but sometimes it has 29.
The year when February has
29 days is called a leap year.

How many days does April have?
Do you know? It has thirty.

There is a saying that helps
me remember the days of
the months. It goes like this.
"Thirty days have September,
April, June and November."

Kevin's birthday is not in the
winter when it is cold. It is in
the summer when it is hot.

Exercises

1. That loaf has ____ on it.

   fold

   mold

   told

2. Do you like your tea hot or ____?

   cold

   old

   mold

3. Holly, ____ your sister's hand!

   bold

   told

   hold

4. Did he ____ the paper?

   fold

   sold

   bold

5. Alex was as ____ as a lion.

   told

   cold

   bold

Stories

I Have a Favorite Month

I have a favorite month. It is not in the summer. The summer months are too hot for me. It is not in the winter, either. January and February are full of wind, ice and cold. No, I like April. April is the first full month of spring. Many flowers bloom in April. The flowers are very beautiful in the spring.

The Oldest Girl

In my house there are three girls. I have an older sister and a younger sister. My older sister is named Lily and my younger sister is named Sarah. Lily, the oldest, takes very good care of us. She helps our mother make meals, and she helps take care of Sarah. (Sarah is still a baby.) Sometimes I wish I were the oldest girl, but it would be hard too!

Questions

1. February is in the ____.

   fall
   winter
   spring
   summer

2. January and February can be full of ____.

   flowers
   heat
   ice

3. Which of these months is in the spring?

   January
   February
   April

4. Who helps her mother the most?

   the oldest
   the baby
   Sarah

5. Is the storyteller the youngest sister?

   yes
   no

ea

head	bread	heather
tread	breath	pleasant
lead	dread	feather
deaf	instead	weather
read	leather	sweater
ready	health	heaven

At the head, four men blew trumpets as the army tread into the camp.

Reading

Have you read this book about
peacocks? Peacocks are birds
with very fancy tail feathers.
This book says that peacock
feathers are sometimes put in hats!

What is a peasant?
A peasant is a poor farmer.

In the winter, Ron wears a
sweater. You can wear a sweater
over your shirt to keep you warm.

Tim has heather growing in
his backyard. Heather is a
plant that grows in masses.
The leaves of heather are
green in the winter and the
flowers are pink when they
blossom in spring.

To make bread, you need
flour, salt, water and leaven.
Leaven makes the bread rise.
Without leaven, the bread is flat.

Two ways to read 'ea'

leak
tread
bread
head
leaf
deaf
east
feather
peach
near
instead
ear
peak
death
speak
weather

Exercises

1. Heather ate the ____.

    breath
    dread
    bread

2. I want tea ____ of coffee.

    instead
    ready
    heaven

3. Because the ____ was bad, we could not swim.

    sweater
    weather
    head

4. It was so cold, I could see my ____.

    breath
    death
    lead

5. The king's ____ was rich and great.

    head
    health
    realm

Riddles

1. I come from the sun,
   But not from the snow.
   If the pot boils,
   You put me on low.

   bread
   heat
   head

2. You can see me in the cold,
   But you can't when it's hot;
   I warm hands in the winter,
   But cool hot soup from a pot.

   bread
   meat
   breath

3. I drip from pipes,
   To Don's distress.
   He needs some wipes
   To clean the mess!

   peasant
   leak
   feather

Stories

The Weather

Everyone seems to complain about the weather. We talk about it as if there were nothing else to talk about. In summer someone will say, "It's scorching hot today! This Philadelphia weather is really bad." In winter, someone else will say, "I heard it's 72 degrees in Florida. I think I'll move there when I get old." Too hot, too cold, too rainy, too dry, too windy, too still. We have nothing good to say about the weather.

Some Like It Hot

My brother Henry likes the summer. He thinks that the winter is too cold, and he does not like to play in the snow very much. He is looking forward to July because then it will be summer, but I am dreading the summer.

Questions

1. Everyone seems to complain about the ____.

    Philadelphia
    Florida
    weather

2. In summer someone will say ____.

    it is too hot
    it is too cold
    it is good weather

3. Why do we complain about the weather?

    The weather is really too hot.
    The weather is really too cold.
    People like to complain.

4. July is in the ____.

    fall
    winter
    spring
    summer

5. Henry is looking forward to ____.

    the winter
    April
    July

Poetry

If I'd As Much Money As I Could Spend

If I'd as much money as I could spend,
I never would cry, "Old chairs to **mend**!
Old chairs to mend! Old chairs to mend!"
I never would cry, "Old chairs to mend!"

If I'd as much money as I could tell,
I never would cry, "Old clothes to sell!
Old clothes to sell! Old clothes to sell!"
I never would cry, "Old clothes to sell!"

Questions

1. Does the speaker in this reading have a lot of money?

   yes
   no

2. The word "mend" means ____. (The word is printed in bold in the reading.)

   sit on
   spend
   fix

3. "Old clothes to sell" is something that ____.

   rich people would say
   old people would say
   poor people would say

ought

fought sought
thought brought
bought ought

The knights in the camp fought long and hard.

Reading

Who bought these socks?
The socks are orange, yellow,
blue and green.

Was the bird's head orange or red?
The head of the bird that the man
brought to class was orange.

What did the boys do?
The boys fought over
the orange and yellow pencils.

He still has the books.
Bob ought to take the
blue book back to him.

We sought for the orange shirt.
They found the orange shirt
under the desk.

Tom bought a boat with an orange sail.
The boat had two orange sails.

Elsa brought her doll downstairs
and put it on the sofa. Her mother's
friend bought the doll as a present.

Exercises

1. The knights ____ with swords.
   bought
   fought
   sought

2. Tom ____ a new bike.
   thought
   bought
   fought

3. Steve ____ a way out, but could find none.
   sought
   brought
   wrought

4. Boys and girls ____ to obey their mother and father.
   thought
   wrought
   ought

5. Rebecca ____ she knew the man, but she did not.
   thought
   brought
   ought

6. Michael threw a stick and his dog ____ it back.

   bought

   thought

   brought

7. The fence was made of ____ iron.

   sought

   thought

   wrought

8. Sam's camping trip showed no ____; he had no light, no tent and no food.

   bought

   forethought

   wrought

9. Elsa's mother ____ a new bag for her books.

   sought

   wrought

   bought

10. I ____ he was coming with us, but he isn't.

    thought

    bought

    brought

Stories

Mother and Sister

This is Samuel's drawing. He is almost nine and likes to draw the things he sees. When his baby sister Anna was born, Samuel often saw his mommy holding his sister in her arms. Samuel then got an idea to draw his mommy and the baby. The baby is smiling in the picture because he sees Anna smile a lot. When his sister Elsa talks to her, Anna smiles. When her daddy picks her up and makes her stand on his lap, she smiles and will even let out a giggle.

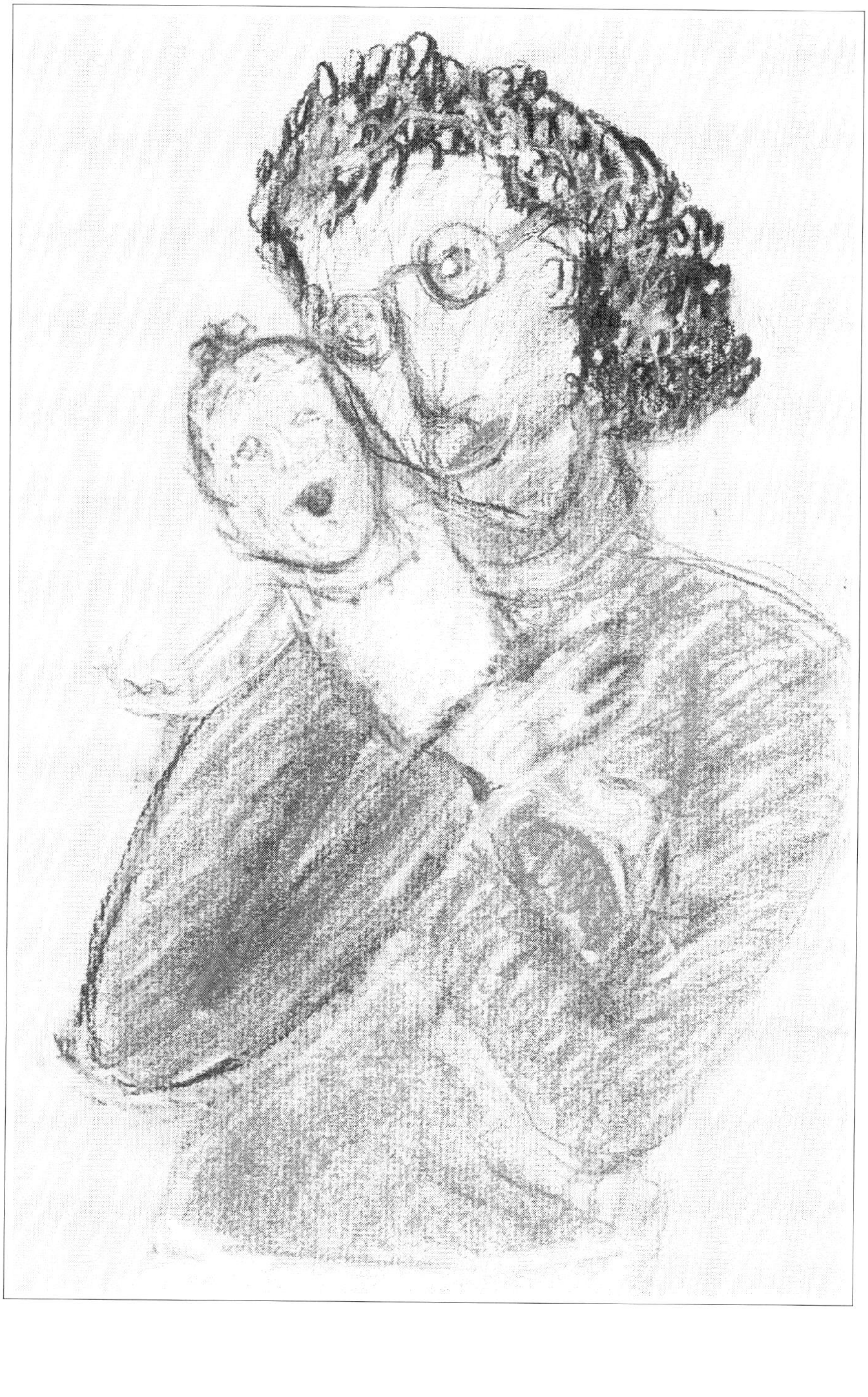

Samantha's Doll

Samantha's daddy bought a new doll. Now she has three dolls. She plays with them in the morning. She likes to sit next to them on the sofa. Yesterday Samantha brought one of her dolls downstairs and put it on the sofa next to her. She put her arms around them just as her mommy and daddy put their arms around her.

The Brothers Fought

Every morning the four brothers fought. They fought over who could sit on the sofa next to Daddy. Now they cannot sit next to Daddy. Because they fought, only their baby sister Lizzy can sit next to Daddy.

Questions

1. How many dolls does Samantha have?

    one

    two

    three

2. How many brothers does Lizzy have?

    none

    two

    four

3. Who got to sit next to Daddy?

    the oldest

    the youngest boy

    the baby girl

4. Does Samuel's sister smile a lot?

    yes

    no

5. Does Anna's mother hold her often?

    yes

    no

oo

too	loon	stoop
smooth	soon	droop
moon	food	groove
roof	goose	shoot
room	spoon	ooze

The bird's feathers were smooth.

Reading

The room was very spacious
and could fit a sofa, two
chairs, a writing desk
and a table.

The flowers in the vase
were drooping. They
needed some water.

Soon the food in our satchels
was gone. We thought we
had brought enough food for the
trip, but we were wrong.

His wound began to ooze.
Should he put some ointment
on it?

I want to see the moon,
too, through the telescope.

Eat this food with a spoon.
If you don't, it will get
very messy.

The goose's feathers began
to droop. They felt very smooth.

Exercises

1. The sap ____ from the pine tree.

   shoot
   oozed
   drooped

2. Neil Armstrong was the first person on the ____.

   moon
   shoot
   room

3. We had Anna's birthday party in the big ____.

   room
   too
   ooze

4. The freshly cut flowers began to ____ in the sun.

   ooze
   smooth
   droop

5. In the winter Sally's skin is dry, but in the summer it is ____.

   too
   ooze
   smooth

6. Roof
   crate
   house
   desk

7. Moon
   sky
   food
   grass

8. Roost
   hen
   pack
   list

9. Shoot
   smooth
   run
   gun

10. Goose
    bird
    house
    lake

Stories

The Moon

Look how bright the moon is tonight! It is a full moon. It looks like the moon is getting bigger and smaller, but it is really the same size. It looks bigger or smaller when more or less of it is lit up by the sun.

When you cannot see the moon, it is called a new moon. When it is all lit up, it is very bright, and it is called a full moon. When the moon looks like it is getting bigger, it is "waxing." When it looks like it is getting smaller, it is "waning." It takes almost a month for the moon to wax and wane. It is fun to look at the sky at night!

Questions

1. Does the moon really get bigger and smaller?

    yes

    no

2. When the moon is all dark, it is called a ____.

    new moon

    waxing moon

    full moon

3. When the moon is getting bigger, we say it is ____.

    full

    waxing

    waning

4. When the moon is getting smaller, we say it is ____.

    full

    waxing

    waning

5. It takes a ____ for the moon to wax and wane.

    day

    month

    year

Poetry

Rain

Rain, rain, go away,
Come again another day;
Little Johnny wants to play.

Questions

1. In the poem "Rain," what does the speaker want?

    the rain to stop
    to play
    to sing

2. Who wants to play?

    a big boy
    a man
    Johnny

le

puddle riddle nibble
little fiddle crackle
giggle bubble purple
juggle trickle simple
ripple waffle dimple

Look at the ripples that the rowers are making!

Reading

Dip the paddles in the sea!
We have two paddles to row
the boat across the sea.

Karen stepped across the
puddle. She did not want
to get muddy in the puddle.

He said there was a bear
at the circus that could juggle.
He said that it juggled sticks on fire.

Did you hear Sam and J. J.
giggle across the room?
Why were they giggling?

I like to blow bubbles.
The bubbles float up.

My uncle plays the fiddle.
Both my uncle and aunt
play the fiddle.

Our little sister wiggled in her seat,
and when we told her to be still,
she started to giggle.

Exercises

1. He burned the ____ until midnight.

    bottle
    apple
    candle

2. His aunt and ____ came to the birthday party.

    candle
    simple
    uncle

3. John ate the red ____ for dessert.

    able
    bottle
    apple

4. Was he ____ to finish his homework?

    people
    able
    bottle

5. The ____ waited in line for hours to buy a ticket.

    people
    able
    bottle

Stories

Blowing Bubbles

My little sister Alice is three years old. She drinks her milk out of a straw. Sometimes she blows into the straw to make bubbles in the milk. It makes a loud gurgling sound that is very annoying. Then Alice gives out a loud giggle. When she giggles, dimples appear in her cheeks in chin. She is very cute when she giggles, but she should not be making bubbles in her milk!

The Jugglers

Every May we go to a fair. At the fair, there are two jugglers. Whenever I try to juggle, it is very hard, but these jugglers make it seem simple. It is a fun show to watch. They juggle all colors of balls: red, green, purple and orange. And they juggle other things, too: eggs, torches, and tennis rackets. Once, one of them juggled three fiddles! It was amazing to see.

Questions

1. Alice drinks milk ____.

    from a bottle
    from a bowl
    with a straw

2. The gurgling sound Alice makes is ____.

    loud
    nice
    polite

3. Should Alice be blowing bubbles?

    yes
    no

4. How many jugglers are at the fair?

    one
    two
    three

5. What did they once juggle?

    oranges
    fiddles
    clubs

mb

thumb   climb
lamb   comb
bomb   limb
numb   tomb
plumber   womb
dumb   crumb

See the lamb next to its mother ewe!

Reading

I hit my thumb twice. Did you
break it? I doubt it. It's numb,
but I doubt I broke it.

Please comb your hair! It looks
as if you just climbed out of bed.

Did the plumber fix the pipes?
I doubt it. The pipes were very
old and the plumber had a
hard time fixing them.

See the lambs? The lambs
are in the field grazing.

We climbed the hills and
looked down. It was a big
climb and we were very high up.

You should never call anyone
dumb. It is not nice to say
someone is dumb.

If you owe money you are
in debt. Are you in debt?
I doubt it.

Exercises

1. It is on a person's hand.

    lamb
    bomb
    thumb

2. You do it to your hair.

    womb
    comb
    bomb

3. It means "grave."

    plumber
    tomb
    numb

4. It is an arm or a leg.

    numb
    climb
    limb

5. It is a person who works with pipes.

    crumb
    lamb
    plumber

Stories

The Clogged Drain

Last week, we had a problem in our bathroom sink. The sink was clogged, and we couldn't unclog it. When the water was running, it would fill up the sink and wouldn't go down the train.

On Wednesday, we called a plumber to unclog the drain. It took the plumber three hours to fix the problem! He said that there was too much hair in the drain. He told us that when we comb our hair, we should not let any get into the sink!

In Debt

Two years ago I lent my brother Bob fifty dollars. He still hasn't paid me back. He is in debt! Until he pays me back, he is fifty dollars in debt. I really doubt that he will pay me back. I should talk to Bob about the money he owes me.

Questions

1. When the water was running, what happened?

   The water went down the drain.
   The drain got unclogged.
   The sink filled up.

2. How long did it take the plumber to fix the problem?

   a short time
   three hours
   all day

3. What was clogging the sink?

   combs
   hair
   water

4. Has Bob paid his brother back?

   yes
   no

5. What does Bob need to do if he does not want to be in debt?

   talk to their father
   pay his brother back
   go to the bank

Poetry

Diddle Diddle Dumpling

Diddle diddle dumpling, my son John
Went to bed with his **breeches** on,
One **stocking** off, and one stocking on;
Diddle diddle dumpling, my son John.

Questions

1. What does the word "breeches" mean? (The word is printed in bold in the reading.)

    a bed

    pants

    socks

2. What does the word "stocking" mean? (The word is printed in bold in the reading.)

    woman's clothing

    arm

    a long sock

3. Who could be talking in the poem?

    John's brother

    John's mother

    John's friend

kn

knot	knee	knit
know	knell	knight
knew	knoll	knave
knock	knife	knob

The three knights stood with spears in hand.

Reading

Did you knock at the door?
It is rude to enter without
knocking.

I can tie a knot.
Can you tie a knot?

I heard the knell of the bell.
The knell was very loud.

We climbed the knoll
and looked down. Do you
think you will fall? I doubt it.

Is that knife clean? I doubt
it. It has green stuff on it.

Mrs. Mason was on the sofa
knitting a sock. She had knit
five socks that week with
brown and red yarn.

They were so scared that
their knees were knocking.

I grabbed the knob of the
door and opened it. I did not
knock.

Exercises

1. Ouch! I hit my ____!

   knot
   knee
   knew

2. Did you cut it with a ____?

   knit
   knight
   knife

3. He put his hand on the ____ to open the door.

   knock
   knew
   knob

4. Jeremy didn't ____ who was coming for dinner.

   knell
   knave
   know

5. Do you like to ____ socks?

   knit
   knock
   knoll

Stories

Nancy Learns to Knit

My aunt is teaching me how to knit! (She is my mother's older sister.) My grandmother's birthday is next month, and I want to knit a hat for her. It is not easy to learn how to knit. The yarn gets tangled. I got a knot in my yarn five times! But my aunt knows how to fix the knots in the yarn. With her help, I think I can finish the hat.

The Knight and His Knave

I read an old story the other day. It was about a young man named Gareth. In the story, Gareth has to work in the kitchen as a knave. Then he goes to fight a bad knight. He jousts with the bad knight and knocks him off his horse. Then Gareth becomes a knight himself.

I thought it was a good story. Maybe you will read it one day!

Questions

1. The hat is for ____.

   Nancy's aunt
   Nancy's mother
   Nancy's grandmother

2. ____ kept getting in the yarn.

   Knaves
   Knives
   Knots

3. Who is helping Nancy learn to knit?

   the aunt
   the mother
   the grandmother

4. Where does Gareth have to work as a knave?

   with the king
   in the kitchen
   with a good knight

5. Does Gareth win his fight?

   yes
   no

wr

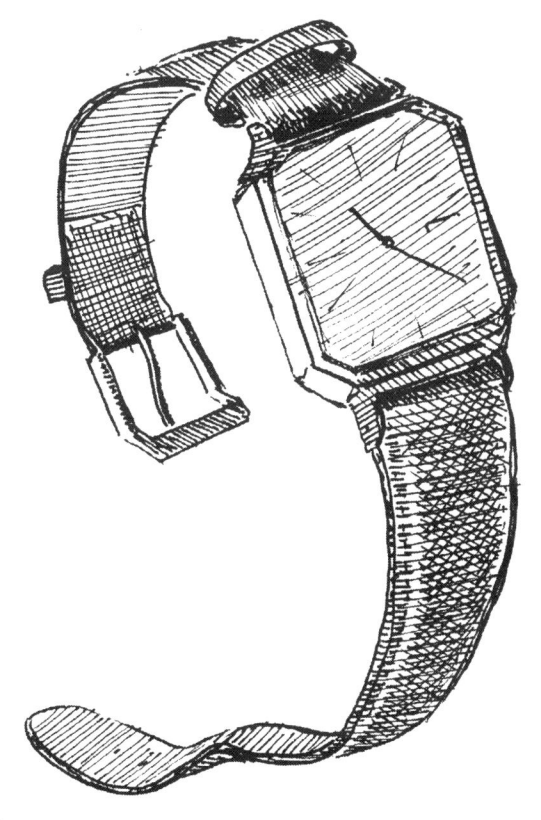

wrist
wrath
wreck
wren
wrench
wrap
wrapper

wrong
writhe
wry
awry
write
wrote
written

Sam wore a watch on his wrist.

Reading

Pick up the knife with care.
The knife is very sharp
and might cut your hand.

I saw a wren sitting on a
branch of a tree. The wren
had an insect in its beak.

She had to wrap the gift
twice. Did she wrap the gift
with red or green paper?

The snake in the grass writhed
into the brush. If Sarah sees it
writhe, she will scream!

The knock at the door was loud
and awoke the sleeping baby.
Who was knocking at the door?

I doubt he can climb that hill
with his bike. The hill is very
steep and covered with ice.

Exercises

1. My brother needed a ____ to cut the string.

    write
    knife
    knob

2. Rachel ____ a letter to her brother.

    wrote
    wrap
    wren

3. Martha put the bracelet on her ____.

    written
    wrong
    wrist

4. Did Sam ____ his brother was at the door?

    knock
    knew
    know

5. The farmer had five ____ on his farm.

    climbs
    lambs
    thumbs

Stories

It Was Wrong

I saw a boy hitting a bird's nest, which was in a bush on our porch. The birds were chirping for their mother. What made the boy do it? My father saw him do it, and told him to stop. It was wrong of him to hit the nest. He might have killed the baby birds!

The Letter

Dear Erik,

Thank you for your last letter. It was long, but mine will be short, since I do not have much to write. I heard that your parents gave you a new dog for your birthday—a collie. What a great pet! My birthday was last week. My father bought me a blue watch. It was too big for my wrist, though, so I will have to get another band.

Do you plan to come to Philadelphia soon? It would be great to see you!

Your friend,
Ted

Questions

1. Where was the birds' nest?

    in a bush

    in a tree

    under the porch

2. What were the baby birds doing?

    chirping

    eating

    flying

3. Did the boy do a good thing?

    yes

    no

4. What did Erik get for his birthday?

    a collie

    a poodle

    a cat

5. What did Ted get for his birthday?

    a pet

    a dog

    a watch

Poetry

The City Mouse and the Garden Mouse
By Christina Rossetti

The city mouse lives in a house—
The garden mouse lives in a **bower**;
He's friendly with the frogs and toads,
And sees the pretty plants in flower.

The city mouse eats bread and cheese—
The garden mouse eats what he can;
We will not grudge him seeds and stocks,
Poor little timid furry man.

Questions

1. The word "bower" sounds most like ____.
   (The word is printed in bold in the poem.)

   grow
   blow
   flour

2. The word "bower" means ____.

   a shady spot
   an animal
   a house

3. Who or what is the "poor little timid furry man" in the last line of the poem?

   the city mouse
   the garden mouse
   a man visiting the garden

tion

sta tion
mo tion
na tion
lo tion
ac tion
po tion

cre a tion
sal va tion
pol lu tion
af fec tion
ad di tion
sub trac tion

Did the train arrive at the station on time?

Reading

The car is in motion.
Do not open the door
when the car is in motion.

There is a lot of action
in those sports. There is a lot of
action in tennis, swimming,
basketball, and fencing.

"Does Sarah know subtraction
and addition?" Noah asked. "Yes,"
Ben answered. "She knows both
subtraction and addition."

My dad asked directions to the
zoo. The directions were clear,
but we had a hard time
finding the zoo.

I asked, "Did the boys swim?"
"No," he answered. "The stream
has a lot of pollution."

When there is not much food
in a nation, there may be a
ration. Foods like butter
may be rationed.

Exercises

1. The stream had rusty cans, bottles, and other ____.
   addition
   pollution
   ration

2. I need sun tan ____ to protect it from the sun.
   lotion
   nation
   addition

3. Baseball does not have a lot of ____.
   nation
   action
   subtraction

4. We took a train to the next ____.
   potion
   traction
   station

5. The United States is a big ____.
   dictation
   motion
   nation

Stories

Alex's New Sister

Two years ago, I had no brothers or sisters. Then my mom and dad told me that they were thinking about an adoption. I didn't know what an adoption was. They told me that an adoption is taking a boy or a girl with no mother or father into the family. Soon, they adopted a little girl, and they named her Abby. Abby was a nice addition to the family! When I first saw her with my mom and dad at the train station, I knew she would be a good little sister!

Emily Visits an Old Station

Last Friday, we went to visit an old train station. It isn't used anymore. When the station was used, the trains were all run on steam. There was an old steam train sitting in the station for us to look at. (They used steam to put the wheels in motion. That is why they are called steam trains.) Old trains are fun to look at, but I am glad that they are not used anymore! They were very loud and made a lot of pollution.

Questions

1. After the adoption, Alex had a new ____!
   brother
   sister
   mother

2. Where did Alex first see Abby?
   at the train station
   in the car
   at home

3. Was the station that Emily visited still being used?
   yes
   no

4. Old trains used ____ to put the wheels in motion.
   gas
   steam
   electric power

5. What does the story say about old trains?
   They are not loud.
   They are still used.
   They made pollution.

wh

wheat	who	whiskers
what	whom	whet
which	whose	while
when	where	whole
why	wheel	whistle

What a tasty loaf of whole-wheat bread!

Reading

When will we go to the
wharf by the sea? What will
we find at the wharf?

I like whole-wheat bread.
Whole-wheat bread has
a hearty taste.

John whistled while we worked.
I did not like his whistling
because it was out of tune.

That piece of whole-wheat
bread whet my appetite! I would
like to have a cheese sandwich
with whole-wheat bread.

Why did the wheel fall off
the bike? Wasn't it screwed
on right?

Does Mr. Smith work at the
wharf? I thought he did.

When will dinner be
ready? I will clean my
room while I wait.

Exercises

1. ____ painting did you like best?

    Wheel
    Which
    When

2. Did Joan eat the ____ cake?

    whose
    whom
    whole

3. Do you ____ while you work?

    wheat
    wheels
    whistle

4. Leo ____ his knife on the sharpening stone.

    whet
    whole
    who

5. Do you prefer ____ or oats?

    wheel
    wheat
    whiskers

Stories

A Loaf of Bread

There are many kinds of bread. I like whole-wheat, rye, and oat bread. But I like sourdough bread the best. A lot of people do not like sourdough bread. They say it has a funny taste. But I think that they are wrong. It has a great taste. I like bread with all sorts of things, but the best way to eat it is plain with butter!

At the Wharf

My father works at the wharf. When he comes home he often tells us about his day. On Tuesday he told a funny story about a man who had fallen in the water and cried out, "Shark! Shark!" The other men at the wharf heard him and looked down, but saw nothing. "Where's the shark?" The man said not to waste time, but to lift him onto the dock. This they did. The man then said, looking down, "There it is!" But it did not move like a shark. It wasn't a shark at all! It was one of the workers at the wharf who was wearing flippers while swimming. The flippers looked like the fins of a shark.

Questions

1. What kind of bread does the storyteller like best?

   white
   whole-wheat
   sourdough

2. What do some people say about sourdough bread?

   It has a funny taste.
   It is less healthy than white bread.
   It is best with peanut butter.

3. How does the storyteller like to eat sourdough bread?

   with jam
   with cheese
   with butter

4. Why was the man scared?

   He could not swim.
   He thought he saw a shark.
   The water was too cold.

5. Was there really a shark in the water?

   yes
   no

ies

babies
cookies
bunnies
brownies
goodies
ditties
patties
berries

ponies
posies
puppies
marries
candies
ladies
cities
stories

I see five cookies on that plate.

Reading

Do you know what posies
are? A posy is a little
bouquet of flowers.

Do you play a little game
called "Ring-a-round a rosy"?
These are the words we say:

"Ring-a-round a rosy,
A pocket full of posies,
Ashes! Ashes!
We all fall down."

Do you like the city?
There is a lot to see in
the city, but I get
tired quickly.

What goodies did your sister
make for tea? Did she make
cookies and brownies?

Babies are so funny!
Sometimes they like to talk,
even though they are not
saying anything.

Exercises

1. Did the children ride the ____?
   candies
   ponies
   cities

2. I like eating ice cream with ____ on top!
   berries
   ladies
   stories

3. Young dogs are called ____.
   berries
   goodies
   puppies

4. Does your dad like to tell you ____?
   brownies
   candies
   stories

5. Jim always hums ____ to himself.
   ditties
   marries
   babies

Stories

The Blueberry Cookies

On Monday, Mother had Mrs. O'Henry over for tea. She made cookies just for her. The cookbook said that the cookies would be good with some berries. Mother had blueberries in the house, so she put them in. She did not know that Mrs. O'Henry does not like blueberries!

Mrs. O'Henry was very nice and did not tell Mother, but she only ate a little bite of the cookies. "Joan and Teddy can have the cookies," she said. Mother felt bad, but Henry and I were happy. We were glad we could eat the cookies!

Questions

1. Joan and Teddy's mother made ____.

   brownies

   candies

   cookies

2. What kind of berries did she put in?

   strawberries

   blueberries

   blackberries

3. Does Mrs. O'Henry like blueberries?

   yes

   no

4. Did Mrs. O'Henry say that she didn't like the cookies?

   yes

   no

5. Why were Joan and Henry happy?

   because Mrs. O'Henry was nice to their mother

   because there were no brownies on the table

   because they could eat the cookies

ss

hiss
class
pass
grass
kiss
miss

mess
less
fuss
boss
toss
dress

Did the snake hiss
when the bird took it in its beak?

Reading

My baby sister likes to
get kisses. My mother kisses
her each morning and night.

I miss going to my uncle's
house on Saturdays. We play
outside. I toss a ball to him
and he tosses it back to me.

Did all the students in the
class pass the test? I think
they all did pass the test.

I will try not to fuss when I
don't get my way. My mother
and father told me not to fuss
or make faces when I don't
get what I want.

It was no loss when I lost
my rusty bike. I needed
a new one anyway.

Could I pass this way?
The hill is steep but is also
shorter and may take less time.

Exercises

1. The baby was ____.

   rising
   fusing
   fussing

2. It was a great ____ to the family.

   lose
   loss
   boss

3. Your ____ is beautiful!

   toss
   dross
   dress

4. The cars were ____ us on the road.

   pacing
   passing
   lasting

5. The ____ were eating the cheese!

   mice
   miss
   spice

Stories

A Snake in the Grass

I once saw a snake in the grass. I was walking along a trail at Cape May Point, when I saw the thick black snake slither in front of me. I was taken by surprise. It writhed and twisted for a moment and then was gone. It slithered back into the foliage. It left as suddenly as it came.

Noah Passed the Ball

I was tossing a ball back and forth with my brother James, when I threw the ball too hard and it landed in the foliage.

"Where did it go?" James asked.

"In the bushes," I answered.

"Why did you throw it there?"

"I'm sorry. I didn't mean to!" I said.

Questions

1. Was the snake surprising?

    yes

    no

2. What color was the snake?

    brown

    green

    black

3. The snake was ____.

    fast

    slow

    not moving

4. What was the "foliage"?

    bushes

    grasses

    trees

5. Did Noah mean to throw it in the bushes?

    yes

    no

age

voy age
vil lage
cot tage
dam age
stor age
sav age

pas sage
mes sage
man age
gar bage
im age
cab bage

It was a long voyage from England to America.

Reading

It took courage for him
to do that. What did he do?
He took a voyage across
the Atlantic Ocean.

Does she have a cottage
by the ocean. Yes, she
does. She lives at Cape May.

Since Mr. Smith isn't here,
let me leave a message.

Did the storm do any damage
to the ship in its voyage
across the ocean?

How long was the voyage
of the Pilgrims when they
crossed the ocean to America?

Did you hear that sound in
the foliage? I heard a hiss.
I think it might be a snake.

I found a bottle in the ocean.
Was there a message in the
bottle? I doubt it.

Exercises

1. The children visited the old woman's little ____ in the country.

    damage
    message
    cottage

2. It took a lot of ____ for the Pilgrims to take such a long ____ across the deep, wide ocean to America. (Circle two answers)

    cabbage
    courage
    voyage

3. Robinson Crusoe was worried that there were ____ on the island.

    damages
    messages
    savages

4. What _____ do you want me to give your father when I see him?

   voyage
   savage
   message

5. For the first years of his life, William lived in a small _____ in Germany.

   village
   voyage
   courage

Stories

Too Much Stuff!

Next door to where I live, there is an old barn. The barn is used for storage: people leave things to keep there. I think you should only keep nice things, but this barn is full of things that aren't very nice. In fact, most of it looks like garbage. There is a table in the barn that is damaged. It has a lot of scratches, and it only has three legs. It is missing the other leg. I don't know what I would do if I had so many old and damaged things in storage!

The Message

I got a message from my friend Andy today. He said that he went on a voyage with his family to Spain. (He got there last week, but the letter came today.) Andy said the voyage was very long, but the weather in Spain is nice. They are staying in a small village, not a big city.

Questions

1. What is the barn used for?

   keeping cows
   living in
   storage

2. Are all of the things in storage nice?

   yes
   no

3. The table in the barn ____.

   is very nice
   is perfect
   is damaged

4. How did Andy send his message?

   He mailed a letter.
   He sent an email.
   He called his friend.

5. Andy and his family are staying ____.

   in a big city
   in a small village
   in a place with bad weather

cious

spa cious
de li cious
pre cious
gra cious

vi cious
fe ro cious
con scious
lus cious

We looked in awe at the spacious sky.

Reading

We took a walk in our neighborhood and saw a ferocious dog. The woman who was walking it said that it was very friendly, but my friend said that it was vicious.

What do you call this delicious dish? It tastes so good I want the recipe.

The kitchen was spacious enough for the four of us to do some cooking.

Water is very precious in the desert. You do not want to waste it.

The woman made a harsh complaint at the counter, but the man made a gracious reply.

We just ate some luscious chocolate cake.

Exercises

1. The queen wore rubies and other ____ stones.

   precious
   gracious
   vicious

2. The ____ dog bit Tim but not Katie.

   gracious
   vicious
   delicious

3. The room was very ____ and had lots of room for the new chairs.

   spacious
   ferocious
   precious

4. The cake was a ____ dessert.

   vicious
   delicious
   spacious

5. The ____ lion roared.

   precious
   delicious
   ferocious

6. A big room
   delicious
   spacious
   gracious

7. A tasty meal
   delicious
   spacious
   gracious

8. A hungry lion
   vicious
   spacious
   gracious

9. A kind man
   delicious
   spacious
   gracious

10. Rare and costly
    vicious
    precious
    ferocious

Stories

The Cupcake That Carl Didn't Like

I think cupcakes are delicious. But one time I ate a cupcake that I did not like. When was that? Last night. As a gift, Mrs. Smith gave ten cupcakes to our family. I was eager to eat one, and before I took one bite, asked my mom if I could have two. But then I bit into one. It had little bits of orange peel in it. I was nice to Mrs. Smith, but said I could only eat one. I don't think that cupcakes are very delicious when they have bits of orange peel in them.

The Vicious Fight

I went to the zoo last weekend. Something seemed to be happening in the lion's cage. I went over to look, and saw two lions having a vicious fight! I knew that lions can be ferocious animals, like tigers and bears, but I had never seen them like that before. I am glad there is a cage at the zoo to keep them from attacking me.

Questions

1. Does Carl think cupcakes are tasty?

    yes
    no

2. Why did Carl ask for two cupcakes?

    He thought he would like them.
    He wanted to give one to his brother.
    He wanted to be nice to Mrs. Smith.

3. Who brought the cupcakes?

    a brother
    the mom
    Mrs. Smith

4. Carl does not like ____.

    any cupcakes
    his mother's cupcakes
    cupcakes with orange peel

5. What animals were fighting?

    lions
    tigers
    bears

tch

Dutch	patch	hatchet
batch	hutch	catch
ditch	stitch	thatch
latch	fetch	match
watch	pitcher	kitchen

Look at the Dutch woman's clock!

Reading

Will Kathy and Emma make
a batch of cookies to bring
to class? Anna watched them
in the kitchen.

He bought a watch from the
Dutch clockmaker. I have a
clock from the same clockmaker
standing on my hutch.

Look at all of those patches
on his pants! The patches
were sewed with stitches.

Anna is playing fetch with her
dog. Watch the dog fetch the stick!

John threw out the blue pitcher
that was sitting on the hutch.

When will the ten eggs hatch?
If the hen sits on them for a few
weeks, they will hatch.

We worked in the pumpkin
patch for hours this afternoon.

Exercises

1. Did the dog ____ the stick?
   fetch
   patch
   hutch

2. We dug a ____ in our backyard.
   hutch
   fetch
   ditch

3. Did you ____ the bigger boys play?
   hutch
   watch
   latch

4. Did Mother ____ the rip in your pants?
   stitch
   watch
   hutch

5. Did Jenny ____ the high ball?
   match
   watch
   catch

6. A long hole in the ground

   match
   hutch
   ditch

7. Something used to lock or fasten a door

   fetch
   match
   latch

8. A short, thin stick used to light a fire

   fetch
   match
   hutch

9. A shelf or cabinet where dishes are stored

   stitch
   hutch
   match

10. To get or go after

    fetch
    ditch
    match

Riddle

We played ball in Mother's garden.
The pumpkins made it hard to catch,
For when the batter hit the ball,
The catcher tripped in the radish ____.

Stories

Anna's Cookies

Yesterday I baked two batches of cookies. (Sometimes I only make one batch, but then they are gone too soon.) When they were baking, I left the kitchen. I forgot about them until I smelled them from upstairs. I ran down just in time to take them out. My family said they were very good.

Too Salty

This pasta tastes very good, but it is a little salty. It makes me thirsty. Can you please fetch a pitcher of water? There is one on the hutch in the kitchen.

Questions

1. How many batches did Anna make?
   one
   two
   three

2. Where was Anna when the cookies were baking?
   She went outside.
   She went upstairs.
   She stayed in the kitchen.

3. Did Anna get her cookies out on time?
   yes
   no

4. Too much salt makes one ____.
   hungry
   thirsty
   tasty

5. Where is the pitcher of water?
   in the kitchen
   in the dining room
   on a counter

dge

fudge	hedge	ridge
budge	dodge	trudge
judge	badge	porridge
edge	wedge	bridge

The wedge of cheese was full of holes.

Reading

We bought some fudge
in town. The fudge was
delicious!

Where did you get that
wedge of cheese? It is
a very big wedge.

The three tired boys
trudged through the snow.

I think this porridge needs a
smidgen more salt. I will
put it in the pot.

I tried harder and harder
to open the door, but it
would not budge.

What does "dodge" mean?
It means to duck or to move
so that something misses you.

A judge is someone who decides
something important. At a big
spelling bee, there will be a judge.

Exercises

1. The firefighter wore a shiny ____.

   fudge
   badge
   trudge

2. The top ____ of this paper is ripped.

   edge
   fudge
   dodge

3. Do ____ in England still wear wigs?

   judges
   smidgen
   porridge

4. The baby stuck its ____ little hand into its mouth.

   ridge
   hedge
   pudgy

5. The leaves on the ____ are green even in winter.

   hedge
   pudgy
   budge

Stories

Dodge ball

On Saturday, I played dodgeball with five friends. Have you ever played dodgeball? It is called "dodgeball" because the players need to run away from the balls. Each team throws balls at the other team, and we need to try not to get hit. It is not painful to get hit, but it means that the other team gets a point.

There were six of us: three on one team and three on the other team. Matt and I chose teams. Matt chose Elizabeth, even though Elizabeth doesn't like the game. Why? Because she can throw the ball well.

Our team lost the game. But I don't mind because I like playing.

Fred's Budgie

My friend Fred has a pet budgie. A budgie is a kind of parrot. Fred's budgie is bright green and has a yellow head. (Many parrots have brightly colored feathers.) Fred's bird can also say some words! I always think it is funny when a parrot repeats words.

Questions

1. Is it painful to get hit by the ball?

    yes

    no

2. How many people were playing dodgeball? (Don't forget to count the storyteller!)

    five

    six

    seven

3. Why did Matt want Elizabeth on his team?

    Elizabeth likes dodgeball.

    Elizabeth can throw the ball well.

    Elizabeth is a fast runner.

4. What colors are the feathers on Fred's bird?

    green and white

    yellow and white

    yellow and green

5. Does Fred's budgie say any words?

    yes

    no

or

motor	actor	tutor
doctor	color	author
razor	tailor	impostor
pastor	manor	spectator
favor	sailor	tractor

The propellor plane had a small motor.

Reading

Jim's pants ripped at the knee
and we had them mended
at the tailor. The tailor did
very fine sewing work.

The sailor had an appetite
for rye bread and swiss cheese.
He went to the bread shop
in town, but forgot his money.

Bob's uncle, who is an actor,
lived in a very old English manor.
He wrote Bob's father a letter
telling him to pay him a visit
and he will answer this week.

Here is a little poem
that I learned this week:

"Tinker, tailor,
Soldier, sailor,
Rich man, poor man,
Beggar man, thief."

Exercises

1. Green is my favorite ____.

    sailor
    color
    tailor

2. The man bought new ____ to shave his beard.

    doctors
    razors
    favors

3. The old plane had a small ____.

    motor
    pastor
    actor

4. After church, Randy talked to his ____.

    color
    doctor
    pastor

5. He brought his ripped pants to the ____.

    tailor
    pastor
    doctor

6. Something that makes food taste good
   flavor
   razor
   manor

7. A teacher
   tailor
   motor
   tutor

8. Someone who fixes or makes clothes
   color
   favor
   tailor

9. Someone who works at sea
   impostor
   sailor
   spectator

10. Someone who acts on stage or in movies
    tutor
    actor
    pastor

Stories

When I Grow Up

What do you want to be when you grow up? A lot of my friends say that they want to be an author or actor. It must be fun, even if it is hard work too.

My cousin wants to be a doctor. Many people want to be doctors, but I think it must be a very tiring job.

I know one thing: I will not become a sailor! I do not like to be at sea, and a sailor must be at sea all day.

The Kind Man

One Tuesday in February, we were driving to Philadelphia. All of a sudden, the motor in our car broke down. I was afraid that we would be stuck on the road, but a kind man who was going to work helped us out. I am glad we did not have to stay by the side of the road for a long time.

What Flavor Was It?

This month, my brother and I got a big box of candies. There were all sorts of colors in the box: red, green, blue, yellow, orange and purple. The purple candies tasted like grapes. The orange candies tasted like oranges. The green candies tasted like apples, and the red and blue were like berries. But we couldn't tell what flavor the yellow candies were! They didn't taste like lemons. They didn't taste like bananas. What flavor could they be?

Questions

1. Where must a sailor work?

   on a high tower
   by a lake
   at sea

2. Why did the family in the car have to stop?

   They ran out of gas.
   The motor in the car broke.
   They were stopped by someone on the road.

3. Who helped the family?

   a friend that they called for help
   someone who was going to work
   a man who was in the car with them

4. How many colors of candies does the last story mention?

   four
   five
   six

5. They did not know what flavor the ____ candies were.

   orange
   yellow
   green

ph

elephant	nephew	graphite
trophy	phantom	gopher
phone	prophet	Christopher
cipher	Sophia	pheasant
Joseph	dolphin	telephone

Christopher, did you know there are elephants in Africa?

Reading

Does Edward have two brothers
named Joseph and Christopher?
No, but he has two brothers
named Thomas and Victor.

Emma and Maddy went
to the Philadelphia Zoo
last Thursday. Did they
see any dolphins? No, but
they did see elephants.

Mr. Smith's nephew Stephen got
on the phone and called the pizza
place down the street. The man
on the phone said that the pizza
would be ready in thirty minutes.

The teacher showed the class
a big graph. The big graph showed
how much money people in America
spend on things like food, clothing,
and gas for the car.

Exercises

1. Did the winner get a ____?
   trophy
   telephone
   nephew

2. We heard the ____ ring three times.
   trophy
   dolphin
   telephone

3. The ____ is a large animal.
   trophy
   elephant
   nephew

4. ____ swim in the sea.
   Nephews
   Trophies
   Dolphins

5. We read about the ____ Elijah last week.
   prophet
   graph
   nephew

6. A large, beautiful bird

   elephant
   dolphin
   pheasant

7. An animal that lives in the sea

   cipher
   graph
   dolphin

8. A machine used for calling people

   telephone
   trophy
   pheasant

9. A large land animal

   telephone
   elephant
   trophy

10. A prize for winning

    phone
    pheasant
    trophy

Stories

The Dolphin

My brother Stephen is a good swimmer. He swims in races every week. Last weekend, he got a prize for swimming so well. He was the fastest racer of the year! He won a big trophy. I saw it at his house last Wednesday.

Stephen's friend Joseph also swims. He is good too, but not as good as Stephen. Joseph calls Stephen "The Dolphin" because he swims so well. I think it is a funny nickname!

Graphite

What is graphite? Graphite is what pencils are made of. It is slippery and gray, and when you write with it, it leaves a gray mark. Graphite is found in rocks. Much graphite comes from China, but some comes from other places.

Sometimes we call the graphite in pencils "lead," but it is not really lead. Lead is a metal, and it is used for other things—not to write with.

Questions

1. Who was the fastest racer of the year

   Joseph
   Stephen
   Stephen's brother

2. Why does Joseph call Stephen "The Dolphin"?

   because of the way he looks
   because of how well he can swim
   because he is smart

3. What color is graphite?

   white
   gray
   brown

4. Where is graphite found?

   in rocks
   on trees
   in the sea

5. What are pencils made of?

   real lead
   graphite
   copper

qu

queen	quiet	quip
quit	quick	quite
quill	square	equal
quest	squire	quiver

Queen Elizabeth of England

Reading

England has a queen, but
Belgium has a king.

Anna and Emma sometimes pretend
that they are queens. They dress up
in long robes and have their brothers
bow down to them.

Did Felicity and Caroline write
that letter with a quill? I thought
that it might take too long to write
a letter that way, but they were quick.

Does Jim know what "quip"
means? I don't think he does, so
I'll tell him. "Quip" means
to make a funny reply.

My teacher said that a square has four
equal sides. How many sides does
a rectangle have? It also has four
sides, but the sides are not all equal.

I told the boys outside to be quiet.
My baby sister was asleep and I
didn't want their noise to wake him up.

Exercises

1. George was so ____ we did not know he was in the room.

    quiet
    quick
    square

2. A ____ has four sides that are ____ in length. (Two answers)

    square
    quit
    equal

3. This ____ of England ruled for twelve years.

    Queen
    quiet
    square

4. Why did he ____ the football team?

    square
    quit
    equal

5. As a runner, Bob is slow, but his brother is ____.

    quite
    quiet
    quick

Stories

Quakers

William Penn was a member of a group called the Quakers. The Quakers were not liked in England. Because the Quakers had a hard time living in England, William Penn wanted to make a new home for them in America. Many Quakers sailed across the sea from England. They came to Pennsylvania, which is a state in America. They built homes in Philadelphia, a city in Pennsylvania. Philadelphia is now a big city.

Pennsylvania was named after William Penn. It means "Penn's woods." "Philadelphia" is a Greek word; it means "brotherly love."

Questions

1. Quakers had a hard time living in ____.

   England
   America
   Pennsylvania

2. How did the Quakers get to America?

   They sailed.
   They went on an airplane.
   They drove.

3. Philadelphia is NOT ____.

   a small town
   in Pennsylvania
   in America

4. Where did Pennsylvania get its name?

   from the pens Quakers used
   from a Greek word
   from William Penn's name

5. What does "Philadelphia" mean in Greek?

   Penn's woods
   brotherly love
   Quaker

silent t

castle	moisten	wrestle
fasten	bustle	hasten
nestle	jostle	rustle
listen	bristle	whistle

We visited a Welsh castle last summer.

Reading

Moisten the envelope and
seal it. If you don't, the letter
might fall out in the bustle
of the mail room.

Do you like to eat chestnuts?
The first time that I had
chestnuts was the time I visited
the castle in Belgium.

Listen! Is someone whistling
or is that the sound of a
bird chirping?

Must you fasten your
seatbelt in Belgium?
I don't know, but fasten
it anyway.

Did he get hurt when he
wrestled his brother? They
should be careful when
wrestling.

The bristles on this brush
were very stiff. I don't know
what the bristles are made of.

Exercises

1. Did you visit the Scottish ____?

    wrestle
    castle
    fasten

2. ____ the stamp and put it on the envelope.

    Bustle
    Castle
    Moisten

3. That ____ is loud!

    whistle
    fasten
    chestnut

4. ____ to this beautiful music.

    Listen
    Fasten
    Chestnut

5. The ____ on the brush are stiff.

    wrestles
    moistens
    bristles

Matching

1. listen — to fight with

2. wrestle — to pay attention to

3. fasten — to make a noise by blowing air between your lips

4. castle — to connect

5. whistle — a large, strong fort

Stories

Christopher's Castle

Christopher has a tree house. It is a little room made out of wood high in a tree in his yard. He climbs into the treehouse with a ladder.

When Christopher plays with his friends, he sometimes pretends that his treehouse is a castle. The children in the castle pull up the ladder so that the other team cannot get in easily. They must climb the tree to enter the fort. When Christopher is in the fort, he sees the others jostling and bustling to try to get in.

Ben's Whistle

More than two hundred years ago, there was a boy named Ben. Once, when he was passing a shop, he saw a toy whistle in the window. He really wanted that whistle! He went into the shop and tried blowing on it. He gave the shop owner all the coins he had in his pockets and went home whistling loudly.

When he got home, though, his brothers and sisters told him to stop blowing on his whistle. They could not stand listening to the loud noise. When they found out how much he paid for it, they laughed at him—he paid four times too much for it!

Ben cried when he found out that he spent too much. He got more sadness from thinking about it than the joy he got from blowing it.

Questions

1. Where did Ben get his whistle?

   in a shop
   from his brother
   from his mother

2. Was Ben happy with his whistle when he walked out of the shop?

   yes
   no

3. Did Ben's brothers and sisters like his whistle?

   yes
   no

4. How much did Ben give the shop owner?

   too much
   too little
   the right amount

5. After he found out how much he had spent, Ben ____.

   was still happy
   did not mind
   became sad

eigh

neigh
eight
sleigh
weigh

neighbor
weight
freight
eighty

The horse gave a loud neigh.

Reading

Did you hear the horse
neigh as it pulled the
sleigh from the stable?

There were eight foreign
students visiting the college.
They were all from France.

The king ruled seventy years.
His reign was very long.

What is your mother's
height? My mother is five
and a half feet tall.

The freight train left
Philadelphia last night
and will arrive in California
in less than a week.

You have lost too much
weight since you were sick.
How much do your weigh now?

Exercises

1. We were frightened by the horse's ____.
   foreign
   neigh
   freight

2. Have you ever driven a ____ across a field of snow?
   neigh
   freight
   sleigh

3. The man at the counter ____ my order of cheese.
   sleighed
   weighed
   neighbor

4. Many ____ visited America last year.
   eight
   weigh
   foreigners

5. What was the ____ train carrying?
   freight
   weight
   foreign

Stories

The Foreign Neighbor

A new neighbor moved in next door. I found out on Tuesday that she is foreign. Her name is Emma, and she is from England. I did not know that English and American people say words in a different ways. But I could still understand her. She said that she used to live in a castle in England, but I think she was teasing me.

Riding in the Sleigh

I rode in a sleigh in the snow on Thursday! It was a lot of fun. There were eight of us in the sleigh, and my uncle was worried that we would weigh too much for the two horses. But the horses did not seem to mind. They pulled us quickly, and they did not neigh.

Questions

1. Where does Emma come from?

2. Does the storyteller think that Emma did live in a castle?

3. Who was worried that there was too much weight for the horses?

4. How many people were in the sleigh?

5. How many horses were pulling the sleigh?

ture

ad ven ture
fur ni ture
na ture
fu ture
fea ture

pic ture
crea ture
mix ture
pas ture
sig na ture

Sledding down a steep hill is an adventure!

Reading

What an adventure it was
going down the snowy hill!

My mother took a picture
of the family as we walked
along the nature trail. She
sent the picture to our
cousins in California.

We enjoyed the nature in
Pennsylvania as we traveled
through the state in our van.

In the future, I will have
to remember to include
my picture and signature
on the papers.

The drink was a mixture
of honey and fruit juice.

Did they get new furniture?
The furniture that they had
before was old and worn out.

Exercises

1. The ____ of the children is hanging on the wall.

    picture
    furniture
    future

2. She could not read the man's ____.

    creature
    signature
    future

3. What an exciting ____!

    adventure
    signature
    nature

4. He liked to camp and hike to enjoy ____.

    picture
    future
    nature

5. If you spend too much now, you will have no money for the ____.

    future
    nature
    creature

Matching

1. mature

    something that will happen

2. creature

    like a grown-up

3. future

    an animal

4. pasture

    an exciting trip

5. adventure

    grassy land

Stories

The Pla ty pus

Do you see the picture of the platypus? The platypus is a very odd-looking creature. It is not a bird, but it lays eggs. It has a bill that makes it look like a duck. It lives near the water. It is funny to see a creature that looks like a mixture of a duck and an otter. It is good to look at the things in nature.

John Hancock's Signature

Look at that signature! It is a very fancy signature. It was written by a man named John Hancock in the year 1776, when America left the British Empire.

John Hancock's signature is so famous that we use his name as a word. If someone asks you for your "John Hancock," it means that they want you to write your signature.

Questions

1. Is the platypus a bird?

2. Does the platypus lay eggs?

3. Does the platypus live close to water?

4. Was John Hancock's signature plain?

5. What did America do in 1776?

ur

curl	nurse	further
churn	purse	murmur
fur	curse	hurry
burp	burst	furry
church	turn	burn

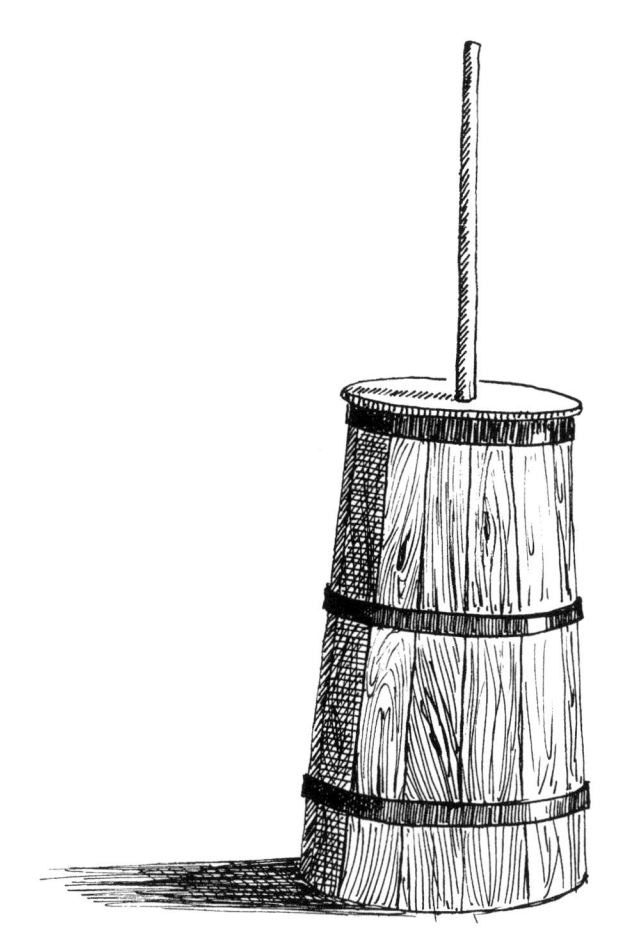

Mary churned the cream until it turned to butter.

Reading

Look at the curls in
that girl's hair. Her
hair was straight, but
turned curly when she
was three.

In the winter, she wore
a brown fur cap to church.

The baby's nurse sang a song,
soft and low. She was trying
to get the baby to sleep.

If you churn the cream
long enough it will turn
into butter.

She took out money from
her purse and gave it to
the beggar in the street.

The urn was finely colored.
It was a beautiful urn.

Exercises

1. The ____ was so fast that we had a hard time steering the boat.
   current
   surprise
   curl

2. Did Samuel ____ you when he came into the room?
   surprise
   usurp
   burst

3. Why are the workers ____ about their boss?
   surprising
   murmuring
   bursting

4. Did the soldier try to ____ the captain's place?
   surprise
   usurp
   burst

5. The pipes ____, and water sprayed everywhere.
   usurped
   turned
   burst

Stories

The Pipes Burst

Last winter was very cold. In January, it was so cold for so long that our pipes froze. There are pipes that carry water to the sinks in our house.

Did you know that when water freezes into ice, it gets bigger? When the water in our pipes froze, it got bigger, and the pipes burst!

Churning Butter

Have you seen a butter churn? A churn has a barrel and a long pole. Inside the barrel, there is cream. A person takes the pole and moves it up and down in the cream. This is called churning. After the cream is churned for a while—about a half hour—it turns into butter and buttermilk!

Questions

1. Water gets ____ when it freezes.

2. In what month did the pipes freeze?

3. What happened to the pipes when the water froze?

4. What is inside the barrel before it is churned?

5. Churning makes ____.

Poetry

The Little Maid
By Lucy Clifford

A little maid went to market,
She went into the town,
And all the things she had to buy
She carefully wrote down.
The coffee, sugar, tea, and rice—
The currant cake for tea,
And then she had to reckon up,
And see how much they'd be.

She sat her down as she came back,
She sat her down to see
What they had cost—the currant cake,
The coffee, and the tea.
She could not make her money right,
And yet, how she did try!
She could not make her money right,
And oh! how she did cry.

She's counting still, my dears, my dears,
She's counting day and night,
But though she counts for years and years,
Shell never make it right.
Shell never make it right—right—right,
Oh! never any more,
Though she sits counting—count—count—count,
Till she is ninety-four.

Questions

1. In the reading, the little maid ____.

   is playing
   stayed at home
   went shopping

2. In the reading, the little maid cannot ____.

   play house
   buy what she wants
   count her money right

3. The reading does NOT say that little maid ____.

   buys meat
   cries
   writes down what she needs to buy

4. From the reading, you know that currant cake ____.

   is hard to buy
   is eaten with tea
   does not cost much money

5. How old is the maid at the end of the poem?

   She is a baby.
   She is very young.
   She is ninety-four years old.

soft g

cage	fringe	gel
huge	barge	gem
page	charge	gym
rage	large	gentle
sage	plunge	giraffe
hinge	dingy	giant

The poor bird is stuck in a cage.

Reading

That is a giant dog. Is it
gentle or is it vicious?
I think it looks gentle.

The diver plunged into
the deep sea.

Someone who is in a rage
is very angry. It is bad
to be in a rage.

The giraffe has a huge
neck. Does any creature
have a neck as large as
a giraffe's?

What do you do at the
gym? Do you lift weights
when you are at the gym?

What does "singe" mean?
If something is singed, it
is a little burnt, but not
too burnt.

Exercises

1. How much did Jim ____ you for the car?
    charge
    large
    barge

2. Joe was very angry. He was ____.
    ranging
    raging
    dingy

3. Did you lift weights at the ____?
    gym
    rage
    hinge

4. ____ live in Africa.
    Pages
    Gentle
    Giraffes

5. The cat's hair was ____ by the fire.
    gym
    dingy
    singed

Stories

Anna Goes to the Zoo

In October I went with my family to the zoo. We saw some small animals and some large animals. The birds were in a big room full of trees and plants. We could see them flying around. They were very colorful.

The snakes were in glass cages. They would be a danger if they had metal cages like the other animals! The giraffes and elephants were not in a cage because they are so large. I was at the zoo once before, but I forgot how large they are. A giraffe's neck is huge! And the elephant has a very long nose. It is called a trunk. I think I like the large animals best of all the creatures we saw at the zoo.

Questions

1. Could Anna see the birds in the big room?

2. What were the snakes kept in?

3. Were the giraffes kept in a cage?

4. An elephant's long nose is called a ____.

5. Does Anna like the small animals best?

oar

oar
roar
boar
soar

hoary
board
coarse
hoarse

The tiger showed its teeth and roared.

Reading

The oars of the boat
were made of wood.

Did you hear how loud
the lion roared? I did not
know what a lion's roar
was so loud.

The birds soared in the sky.

What is a boar? A boar
is a wild pig. Boars can
be very ferocious.

What color should I paint
the wooden boards?

Is this paper smooth or
coarse? I think it is coarse.

My voice is hoarse. I think
I should not sing so loud
for so long.

Exercises

1. Did you see the bird ____?

    sore

    soar

2. That is a strong wooden ____.

    bored

    board

3. Did you hear the tiger ____?

    roar

    coarse

    hoarse

4. You use an ____ to row a boat.

    or

    oar

    ore

5. The ____ pulled the sleigh through the snow.

    horse

    hoarse

Stories

How a Prince Learned to Read
By James Baldwin

A thousand years ago boys and girls did not learn to read. Books were very rare and very precious, and only a few men could read them. Each book was written with a pen or a brush. The pictures were painted by hand, and some of them were very beautiful. A good book would sometimes cost as much as a good house.

In those times there were even some kings who could not read. They thought more of hunting and fighting than of learning.

There was one such king who had four sons: Ethelbald, Ethelbert, Ethelred and Alfred. The three older sons were sturdy, half-grown boys. The youngest, Alfred, was a slender, fair-haired child.

One day when they were with their mother, she showed them a wonderful book that some rich friend had given her. She turned the pages and showed them the strange letters. She showed them the beautiful pictures, and told them how they had been drawn and painted.

They admired the book very much. They had never seen anything like it. "But the best part of the book is the story that it tells," their mother said. "If you could only read, you might learn that story and enjoy it. Now I have a mind to give this book to one of you."

"Will you give it to me, mother?" little Alfred asked.

"I will give it to the one who first learns to read in it," she answered.

"I am sure I would rather have a good bow with arrows," said Ethelred.

"And I would rather have a young hawk that has been trained to hunt," said Ethelbert.

"If I were a priest or a monk," said Ethelbald, "I would learn to read. But I am a prince, and it is foolish for princes to waste their time with such things."

"But I should like to know the story that this book tells," Alfred said.

A few weeks passed by. Then one morning Alfred went into his mother's room with a smiling, joyous face. "Mother," he said, "will you let me see that beautiful book again?"

His mother unlocked her cabinet and took the precious volume from its place of safe keeping.

Alfred opened it with careful fingers. Then he began with the first word on the first page and read the first story aloud without making one mistake.

"O my child, how did you learn to do that?" cried his mother.

"I asked the monk, Brother Felix, to teach me," said Alfred. "And every day since you showed me the book, he has given me a lesson. It was no easy thing to learn these letters and how they are put together to make words. Now, Brother Felix says I can read almost as well as he."

"How wonderful!" his mother said.

"How foolish!" Ethelbald said.

"You will be a good monk when you grow up," Ethelred said with a sneer.

But his mother kissed him and gave him the beautiful book. "The prize is yours, Alfred," she said. "I am sure that whether you grow up to be a monk or a king, you will be a wise and noble man."

Alfred did grow up to become the wisest and noblest king that England ever had. In history he is called Alfred the Great.

Questions

1. Were books cheap a thousand years ago?

2. Which of the four brothers learned how to read?

3. Did he make any mistakes when he was reading to his mother?

4. Who taught Alfred how to read?

5. What did Alfred become when he grew up?

Poems to Memorize

A Chill
By Christina Rossetti

What can lambkins do
All the keen night through?
Nestle by their woolly mother
The careful ewe.

What can nestlings do
In the nightly dew?
Sleep beneath their mother's wing
Till day breaks anew.

If in field or tree
There might only be
Such a warm soft sleeping-place
Found for me!

The Lord Will Provide
By William Cowper

The saints should never be dismayed,
Nor sink in hopeless fear;
For when they least expect his aid,
The Savior will appear.

This Abraham found, he raised the knife,
God saw, and said, "Forbear!
Yon ram shall yield his meaner life,
Behold the victim there."

Once David seemed Saul's certain prey,
But hark! the foe's at hand;
Saul turns his arms another way,
To save the invaded land.

When Jonah sunk beneath the wave
He thought to rise no more;
But God prepared a fish to save,
And bear him to the shore.

Blest proofs of power and grace divine,
That meet us in his word!
May every deep-felt care of mine
Be trusted with the Lord.

Wait for his seasonable aid,
And though it tarry, wait:
The promise may be long-delayed,
But cannot come too late.

A Morning Song
By Isaac Watts

My God, who makes the sun to know
His proper hour to rise;
And, to give light to all below,
Doth send him round the skies:

When from the chambers of the east
His morning race begins,
He never tires, nor stops to rest,
But round the world he shines.

So, like the sun, would I fulfill
The business of the day;
Begin my work betimes, and still
March on my heavenly way.

Give me, O Lord, thy early grace,
Nor let my soul complain
That the young morning of my day
Has all been spent in vain!

The Seasons of the Year
By Isaac Watts

With songs and honours sounding loud
Address the Lord on high;
Over the heavens he spreads his cloud,
And waters veil the sky.

His hoary frost, his fleecy snow
Descend and clothe the ground;
The liquid streams forbear to flow,
In icy fetters bound.

He sends his word and melts the snow,
The fields no longer mourn;
He calls the warmer gales to blow,
And bids the spring return.

The Arrow and the Song
By Henry Wadsworth Longfellow

I shot an arrow into the air,
It fell to earth, I knew not where;
For, so swiftly it flew, the sight
Could not follow it in its flight.

I breathed a song into the air,
It fell to earth, I knew not where;
For who has sight so keen and strong
That it can follow the flight of song?

Long, long afterward, in an oak
I found the arrow, still unbroke;
And the song, from beginning to end,
I found again in the heart of a friend.

There Is But One May in the Year
By Christina Rossetti

There is but one May in the year,
And sometimes May is wet and cold;
There is but one May in the year
Before the year grows old.

Yet though it be the chilliest May,
With least of sun and most of showers,
Its wind and dew, its night and day
Bring up the flowers.

Going Down Hill on a Bicycle
By Henry Charles Beeching

With lifted feet, hands still,
I am poised, and down the hill
Dart, with heedful mind;
The air goes by in a wind.

Swifter and yet more swift,
Till the heart with a mighty lift
Makes the lungs laugh, the throat cry:—
"O bird, see; see, bird, I fly."

"Is this, is this your joy?
O bird, then I, though a boy
For a golden moment share
Your feathery life in air!"

Say, heart, is there aught like this
In a world that is full of bliss?
'Tis more than skating, bound
Steel-shod to the level ground.

Speed slackens now, I float
Awhile in my airy boat;
Till, when the wheels scarce crawl,
My feet to the treadles fall.

Alas, that the longest hill
Must end in a vale; but still,
Who climbs with toil, wheresoe'er,
Shall find wings waiting there.

Typeset
using X͟ǝLᴬTᴇX
in Monotype Plantin Infant